A Monastery Within

A Monastery Within

Tales from the Buddhist Path

GIL FRONSDAL

TRANQUIL BOOKS

*Dedicated to the fellowship of
monks, nuns and lay people
practicing on the Path together*

CONTENTS

Clarity

Wisdom

Epilogue

Preface

I hope you enjoy these tales. They contain some of the insights I learned during my years of Buddhist monastic life. Starting at the age of 24 I spent ten years training in monasteries in America, Japan and Southeast Asia. In the events and adventures of this life I discovered deep and rich connections to others, to myself, and to a life that transcends both. My own stories from this time as a monk are the inspiration for the stories you will find in this book.

After ten years I discovered that the essence of monastic life is not found in the monastery itself, but rather in the qualities of kindness, clarity, and wisdom cultivated through that life. When a person has adequately developed these qualities so that they become guides to further spiritual growth then we say that he or she has created 'a monastery within.'

Imagination is an important aspect of this 'inner monastery.' Imagining ourselves in the shoes of others is needed for cultivating kindness; having a creative vision of how the mind can be purified of its afflictions guides the cultivation of clarity; and imagination adds depth and breadth to wisdom by applying it to the full range of our life experiences. Also, when our imagination is engaged, we often listen and reflect more deeply on the teachings we receive.

These tales were written with the intention of engaging the reader. While I hope the reader enjoys them, I believe that getting the most out of these stories requires a reader's participation in imagining how each story may be relevant to his or her life. Liking or not liking a story is often less useful than imagining situations where the story may provide a helpful perspective. Some of the stories may seem incomplete. It is the task of the reader to complete them.

The tales are loosely organized into the three categories of Buddhist training, usually called Ethics, Meditation, and Wisdom. Here I have called them Kindness, Clarity, and Wisdom because I prefer these words as descriptions of the inner qualities developed along the path of liberation. These three practices give us an inner monastery we can take with us anywhere we go. With kindness we build this inner dwelling place, clarity allows us to inhabit it, and wisdom opens its doors.

Not only do we find our freedom when the doors open wide, it also allows others to benefit from our practice.

My wish is that these stories help open your heart so that kindness, clarity, and wisdom can be your gift to the world.

Introduction

Deep in the distant mountains was a Buddhist monastery that prospered in the way monasteries prosper best. Dedicated monks and nuns had been practicing there for over 300 years. Their freedom and purity of heart attracted many people to Buddhist practice. They were guided by an Abbess who was renowned for her compassion, strength, and spiritual depth. Her effectiveness as the head of the monastery was directly related to the love the residents felt for her.

Everyone who visited the monastery left with some unusual story of how their time there had transformed them. People who had never visited the monastery found some of these stories strange and were often prone to see them as tall tales. But anyone who had ever stayed at the monastery knew the stories to be true. However, what did seem mysterious was the way in which the monastery provided each person exactly the lesson he or she needed most.

In the hope that at least one of these stories might be just the right medicine for people who have never visited the monastery, I have recorded them just as they came to me. Sometimes the shortest path to the truth is through a story.

Kindness

Building the Monastery

A Monastery Within

The Many Ways to Sweep

The Abbess was a most exceptional person. She seemed to always have a smile in her eyes. When she looked at you, it seemed as if she knew you better than you knew yourself. She once told the following story of how she first came the monastery:

"When I was 13, my family would send me up to the mountains around the monastery to collect edible plants for our evening meal. These foraging trips were the only work I enjoyed doing, otherwise I tried every trick I could to avoid work on my family's farm. I was still in school but school had no interest for me; my anger was a welcome barrier to learning anything the teacher was teaching.

"On one of my foraging trips, I would pass by the monastery while the monks and nuns were out sweeping the leaves from the pathways. The first time I saw them working I was mesmerized watching them go about their work. For many months after I would often stop awhile to watch them sweep. They worked silently and with an efficiency that seemed effortless.

"Then one day a monk walked up to me and asked what I was doing in the mountains. The question frightened me and I became defensive. I resented anyone who tried to get to know me. So instead of answering the question I countered by asking what was he doing! The monk smiled and answered that he had been told to sweep and that he was just killing time until he could return to his room for a nap.

"As I walked home later that day I thought about his answer and was glad that he did not seem any different than me. When I was required to do anything my heart was never in it and my attitude was that I was passing time until I could be excused. Taking a nap was certainly preferable.

"The next time I passed by the monastery on one of my foraging trips a nun stopped her sweeping and also asked what I was doing. Again I resented the question. It felt like an intrusion. However, this time I did not feel as scared. Again I deflected the question by asking what she was doing. She answered that she was doing extra work in hope of being assigned to the kitchen which was warm in the winter and always seemed to have one or two extra sweet rice cakes in the cupboard to nibble on.

"Without saying anything I nodded and left to continue my foraging. The nun's answer resonated with me since I too liked to be warm. And eating sweet cakes was one of my favorite activities, second only to sleeping.

"The next time I passed the monastery, another monk asked me the same question. This time I was surprised I was not defensive or resentful of being asked. However, again I deflected the question back to him. He explained that he was sweeping as a spiritual discipline to help him overcome his anger.

"Later as I walked the mountain trail with my bag of plants I felt a kinship with this monk. Like me he had anger. But I was perplexed that he would want to overcome it. For me, my anger protected me.

"A week later I was again outside the monastery watching the monastics sweep. Yet another monk came up to me. When he asked me what I was doing, I mumbled something about collecting plants. I doubt he could hear me: my voice was so faint. But I did muster up enough strength to ask him what he was doing. He replied he was beautifying the monastery so that others could be inspired in their work of spiritual transformation. Before I left him, I glanced down the well-swept paths and realized that part of the reason I was compelled to watch the monks sweep was that they seemed to be transforming the paths into something that made me feel peaceful.

"The next time I stood outside the monastery watching the monastics I was drawn to walk over to yet another nun, and before she could ask me what I was doing, I asked her. She looked at me with kind eyes. And after what seemed like a long but soft silence, she explained that she was sweeping to be of service to all who used the monastery and in practicing this way she hoped to find ultimate peace.

"As I left the monastery that day I thought her answer strange as I didn't understand what she meant by service and by peace. I certainly couldn't see how these had any value for me.

"The next time I visited the monastery was the last time. I had an unfamiliar feeling as I walked up into the mountains. It was a warm glow of gladness in anticipation of what I would find. When I arrived at the monastery I walked up to an old monk who seemed absorbed in his sweeping. I inquired what he was doing.

"As he answered, each of his words washed over me like cleansing water: "Me? I am not doing anything. My self-consciousness was swept away long ago. There is no 'I' that does anything." Before I could respond, he handed me the broom and walked away. I have been here ever since."

The Pilgrimage

At the beginning of every year the Abbess would meet with the new monks and nuns who had joined the monastery the preceding year. "Pack your bags!" she would say, "I'm taking you on a pilgrimage to the holy sites of Buddhism."

Knowing of the pilgrimages to the places in India where the Buddha was born, enlightened, first taught and died, the new monastics couldn't believe their good fortune. Especially because after their first few months in the monastery some of the new residents were bored, some were restless and some were unsure why they were there.

On the day of departure all the older monks and nuns in the monastery stood by the gate to send off the Abbess and the new monastics. Leading the group, the Abbess first took them to a hospital. There they visited the sick.

Then the Abbess took the group to an old age home. The new monastics, many who were quite young, were amazed at the ravages of old age.

The Abbess then took them to a hospice. In the hours there, they spent time with people in all stages of dying. The last few hours were spent in silent vigil with someone who had just died.

The Abbess then led the group back to the monastery. There they visited a nun sick in the infirmary. The new monastics were struck by the sparkle of joy which radiated through the tired eyes of the patient.

Then they went to visit the oldest resident of the monastery, a 96-year-old monk. The group was awed by the love and acceptance that shone forth from the toothless, frail and stooped man.

Next the Abbess took them to the hospice wing of the monastery. Here they were introduced to a nun who, only days away from her death, radiated a palpable peace that lingered within them for hours after.

Finally, the Abbess took the monastics to the meditation hall. When they were all seated, she said, "You have seen the holy sites! These are the sites that motivated the Buddha to Awaken. Once you are awakened, you will no longer be troubled when you encounter old age, sickness and death."

The Brilliant Monk

A young man once came to the monastery to ordain as a monk. He had been raised in relatively fortunate circumstances with easy access to education. Capable, smart and friendly, he succeeded in most everything he set his mind to. Deeply reflective about life, he had studied the teachings of the major religions. In his early twenties he decided not to follow the customary paths of marriage and career.

Leaving behind the life he had known, he ordained at the age of twenty-two and applied himself to the meditation and training the monastery provided. Disciplined, intent, and intelligent he made quick progress in the spiritual practice. Monks and nuns who had been there for years were in awe of how quickly he settled into deep meditation. Within three months of entering the monastery he experienced his first taste of enlightenment.

Immediately, the Abbess grabbed the young monk, dragged him out the front gate and without explanation kicked him out of the monastery.

Later, addressing the residents of the monastery, the Abbess explained, "The new monk's realization was genuine and I am quite happy for him. However, in order for him to mature further along the path of liberation he has to return to the world to experience more of the difficulties and sufferings of life. To understand all the corners of his own heart he has to grapple with issues of livelihood, family, and community life. Furthermore, I expect that someday he will be a great teacher, but for this to happen, he has to understand all these issues so that he can have greater compassion and insight into the lives of his students. For this particular monk, this isn't going to happen in the monastery."

Alternative to Philosophy

After lunch one day, the Abbess and a visiting philosophy professor went for a walk along the river that passed by the monastery. Being a hot day, they eventually sat down to cool off under the shade of a large tree.

The professor asked, "I am interested in learning Buddhist philosophy. Could you tell me some of the fundamental doctrines of your religion?"

"Well," said the Abbess, "I don't think I can help you much. You see, we don't rely on any philosophy at the monastery."

"But," continued the professor, "everyone, consciously or unconsciously, has a philosophy with which they make sense of their life and their purpose."

"It is different in the monastery," replied the Abbess. "At the monastery we rely on awareness not doctrines."

"But," insisted the professor, "you must have a philosophy which explains the importance of being aware."

After pausing to consider how best to respond, the Abbess said, "As we walked along, we were both aware of how hot, sweaty, and tired we had become from our walk. We did not need a philosophy to tell us the benefits of sitting down here in the shade. If you put your hand on a hot

11

stove, you don't need a philosophy to pull the hand away. If a baby is crying from hunger, the need to feed the child is obvious to the parent.

"Buddhist practice does not depend on having a set of doctrines or beliefs. Rather, it depends on being aware of what brings release from suffering. Rather than being taught Buddhist philosophy, at the monastery the monks and nuns are trained to develop an acutely refined awareness. With such sensitivity, ultimate liberation is as natural as sitting down in the shade on a hot day."

Aspirations

Two young men happened to enter the monastery on the same day. One was an aristocrat who had a sense of entitlement. The other was the son of local farmers who had spent his life working on the family farm.

During their entrance interview, the Abbess asked them why they were becoming monks. The aristocrat said that he had come to climb to the highest achievement of human life, to experience the bliss, the glory, and the brilliant light of liberation. The peasant said, "I am poor and unschooled and I have no hope of enlightenment. However, I hope to find the path in the everyday activities of my life. May I see the truth in the food I eat, in the work I do, and in the people I encounter."

Within six months the peasant was graced with liberation. The aristocrat is still striving on courageously.

On Speech

The Abbess taught, "If you want to discover what you don't yet know about yourself, investigate why you say what you say."

Finding the Right Teacher

Many people arrived at the monastery hoping to be admitted to the monastic order. Some were sent away since what they were searching for was not to be found in the monastery.

Once there was a thirty-year-old man who arrived at the monastery feeling exhausted, discouraged and hopeless. He had decided he was no longer capable of living the worldly life. Perhaps, he hoped, the monastery would provide him with a path that would bring him freedom. It was the birth of his second child that had pushed the man over the edge. He could no longer manage to live with the frustration and the demands on his time that family life had become. He was also worn down by his older child's constant pushing the limits of acceptable behavior.

When he came to the monastery he asked that he be put under the care of the Abbess or another great teacher who could help him find peace. He felt encouraged when he was told that this could be arranged. However, first he would have to prepare himself and prove himself to be worthy by sitting alone in meditation for seven days in the small waiting room next to the main entrance of the monastery.

The man cried the first two days. During the third day, he was washed with alternating waves of nausea and fear. The fourth was spent reviewing his life. For the fifth and sixth days he seemed to question every belief he had. By the seventh day he was beginning to feel calmer and certainly more rested than when he had arrived days earlier. At the end of the seventh day he eagerly waited to be admitted into the monastery and to find out who would be his teacher.

When the seven days were over, the Abbess herself came for the man. She congratulated him on completing the solitary retreat.

"Come," said the Abbess, "and I will introduce you to your new teachers. It took awhile, but we have found the ideal people who can help you find both your spiritual strength and freedom."

The Abbess then led the man out the front gate of the monastery. Waiting for him there were his wife and two children. Happy to see them, the man raced out to embrace them.

Then the Abbess declared, "Your wife and two children are your ideal teachers. In your case, nowhere else but in your own family will you find the freedom you are looking for."

With that, the Abbess closed the monastery gate.

Inside Out

An engineer had been a regular and devoted visitor to the monastery for many years. The meditation practice taught at the monastery was the only thing that made sense to him. In fact, the pragmatic logic of the meditation teachings gave him hope that he could overcome his chronic unhappiness and deeply felt pain. He tried all the meditation practices that the Abbess taught him. He began each practice technique with enthusiasm only to have each end with the same frustration. He would encounter a wall he couldn't pass. The closer he came to the wall the more he would recoil back into trying to think his way out of his pain.

Offering him much support, the Abbess encouraged him to relax, trust the practice, and simply feel his inner pain without reacting to it. After many years the Abbess decided a different approach was needed.

During his next visit to the monastery the Abbess told him that if he wanted to continue being her student and to be able to return to the monastery he would have to take on a special practice. Once he had completed the assignment he could then return for deeper teachings. Once more feeling hope, the engineer quickly agreed.

The Abbess said, "For two years I want you to volunteer ten hours a week at the maternity ward at the local hospital. The hospital needs people to hold babies who are born prematurely. If they don't receive enough physical contact, the babies will not grow healthily. When you have finished these two years, please come back to see me."

The man was quite perplexed by this instruction. But because of his trust in the Abbess and his failure to find any relief elsewhere he plunged into volunteering in the maternity ward. He was surprised at how small and fragile the babies were that he held. He would hold them ever so carefully. He would watch their every breath because they all seemed in danger of stopping breathing. He spent a lot of time thinking about how he could more effectively care for the babies he held. But there was nothing more effective than simply holding them against his chest.

After about six months he started feeling something quite new. He started to feel a little spot of warmth and softness in the very center of his being. Since this was a foreign experience that didn't fit any of the ways he thought about himself, he ignored it.

Ignoring it was the best thing he could have done

because it prevented him from interfering with the warmth by thinking about it too much. Over the following months this tender spot grew until it pervaded his body. As it did, the cold, dark wall around his heart slowly relaxed, thawed and dissolved.

When he had completed his two years of volunteering in the maternity ward, the engineer returned to the monastery. The Abbess saw immediately that he was a changed man. He was no longer desperate and he was no longer trying to fit everything he experienced into a conceptual framework. Now he wanted to learn what else the Abbess had to teach.

Giving him a new instruction, the Abbess said to him, "When you meditate, don't think about what is happening. Rather, let your awareness be seated in the tender warmth you feel in your body. If you do this, any meditation practice you do will be fruitful."

The man found this to be true.

On Love

Giving a brief sermon, the Abbess once said, "A hot furnace does not need to be heated. A loving heart does not need to be loved. Being loving is more important than being loved."

The Deer and the Tiger

There was once a monk who was known for his relaxed and trusting nature. No matter what was happening the monk would smile. If circumstances were challenging he would say, "If we can accept how things are and keep a positive attitude, everything we need will unfold on its own."

Once when the monk was on a month long retreat in a hermitage deep in the forest, he witnessed a remarkable interaction between a deer and a tiger. The deer, injured, came stumbling into the clearing in front of the hermitage. Some time later, a tiger wandered into the clearing and saw the wounded deer. The monk held his breath, convinced that the tiger would surely kill and eat the deer. The deer, too, was clearly worried. But as it could no longer walk, the deer accepted its fate, lying very still in the grass. To the monk's surprise the tiger spent the next few days standing guard over the deer until the deer was well enough to wander off again on its own.

The monk was elated at this sight as it seemed to validate his idea that if we could only accept whatever happens fully enough, the boundless goodness of the universe would take care of us.

A few days later lightening struck a neighboring hermitage only a hundred feet away. At first the roof smoldered and smoked. The monk accepted this. The roof then caught on fire. The monk accepted this. Then the rest of the hut started burning. The monk accepted this too. Soon the entire hermitage was gone and the nun who lived there was slightly injured from attempting to battle the flames.

When the Abbess came to investigate the fire, she asked the monk why he didn't go and help put out the fire. In reply, the monk told the story of the tiger and the deer and how it had taught him the importance of surrendering and accepting things in the way the deer had done.

"You fool!" said the Abbess. "Certainly there are times when you should be like the deer, but if you are to be a spiritually mature person, you should also know when to be like the tiger!" With that the Abbess sent the monk away. "Don't come back until you know how to be a tiger. Only when you accept this part of yourself can you understand what it means to accept how things are."

What is Certain

L ocal villagers sometimes believed the Abbess had great powers. Believing the Abbess could predict the future, a local man came to the monastery asking to learn what the future would bring him.

Silently considering this request, the Abbess replied, "Your future will be..." and after a promising pause, she added, "...uncertain."

On Petty Problems

The Abbess once instructed the younger monks and nuns,

"If a fly lands on the back of an ant, it is a big burden for the ant. If a fly lands on the back of an elephant, it is a small thing for the elephant. You will have many challenges in life. It is up to you whether you face them like an ant or an elephant."

Conflict

G iving a talk to the monks and nuns, the Abbess said, "Conflict will always be a part of life in the monastery. Please take your conflicts to be your teachers. Conflicts should not be about winners and losers or between who is right and who is wrong. They should be about discovering your capacity to be strong and to let go, to listen and to speak, to care and to not care, to understand ourselves and others. Please don't fear conflict. Every conflict contains a path to peace. Conflict is the way the heart is trying to find itself."

Exercise

A man came to the Abbess and explained, "I am quite unhappy. I have very little energy for my life. There is nothing I am motivated to do. I have come to you quite desperate. Please take me on as your student and guide me along the Buddhist path. If you would give me some instruction, I am prepared to meditate at least one hour a day."

The Abbess smiled kindly and said, "I am glad you have come here for help. I would be honored to be your teacher. The first thing I want you to do is to spend at least one hour a day vigorously exercising. After you have done this for one year, please come back and I will give you deeper instruction in the spiritual life."

Trusting the Abbess and feeling he had no other choice, the man left committed to the instruction he was given.

The Abbess' assistant who had witnessed the conversation was quite confused by it. "Why," the assistant asked, "didn't you give him instruction in meditation or in other aspects of Buddhist practice? I don't see how exercise is going to answer the man's suffering."

"Well, actually, my instruction was exactly the right thing for him. He has no real spiritual yearning. He has lived a sedentary and lethargic life that has drained him of energy, interest and motivation. Exercise will bring these back to him. When it does, he will discover desires that were buried by his sluggishness. He will not return to the monastery unless he discovers that these desires don't lead to happiness."

Teaching

Most of the monks and nuns at the monastery never became teachers. They were content to continue their practice and way of life. But those who did start the long training to become Buddhist teachers would first have to go through a rigorous preparatory training. The nature of this preparatory training was a carefully guarded secret; only those who had gone through it knew what it entailed. The rumor around the monastery was that the preparatory training was quite difficult, certainly more difficult than the actual teacher training itself.

The preparatory program required practicing generosity. While generosity was something all the monastics practiced, during the preparatory period the instruction was to give in every situation where generosity would be appropriate and anonymous. No one, especially the recipient, was to know who was doing the generous deed.

The preparatory period lasted at least a year. This was to ensure that the monastics had ample time to notice any expectations they might have that their generosity should be reciprocated or acknowledged. It was also long enough that they could see the many consequences of their generosity in the lives of the recipients.

Over time the monk or nun would realize that in being generous, he or she received more benefits than the recipients. When the monastic clearly understood the deep satisfaction of giving freely without any expectation of an exchange, then he or she would be ready to begin training to teach.

The Monastic Alternative

As a teenager she often visited the monastery. She was deeply attracted to the monastic life. The Buddhist path to liberation was what had the most meaning for her. When she became an adult, she planned on joining the monastic order.

However, when she turned 21, her older sister and her sister's husband died in an accident and she became the foster parent for their two young children. In addition, her own parents had become quite old and needed her help. As the only income earner in the family, she had to work long hours every day. She loved to meditate but with all the work and caregiving she had to do, she had no time for it.

Since she was not able to fulfill her aspirations for following the monastic path, she went to the Abbess of the monastery and asked how she could follow the Path with the life she had to live.

The Abbess said that if she couldn't meditate, then the best alternative is to be grateful for everything.

A Monastery Within

Clarity

Dwelling Peacefully Within

Appropriate Instruction

One of the monastery's old monks had become a hermit living deep in the mountains, a two-and-a-half day hike over difficult mountain paths.

Many visitors made the trek to receive advice and teachings from the old man. He was reputed to have an uncanny ability to know just what each visitor needed. Prior to giving instruction the hermit asked that the visitor promise not to tell anyone what advice or instruction he or she received.

After the promise was made the hermit would simply say, "What are you not willing to pay attention to?" This was the only thing he would ever say to anyone seeking his help.

Many visitors were first perplexed by this question. But by the time they had walked the two-and-a-half day trek out of the mountains, they invariably would praise the hermit for giving them just the instruction they needed to hear.

Wisdom and Compassion

When it was time for the monastic community to meditate, the new nun headed for the meditation hall. Placing her shoes on the shoe rack she looked down and saw they were not lined up parallel to each other. This helped her to see that she was slightly distracted due to the excitement of her first day in the monastery. Letting go of her distraction, she looked more carefully at what was in front of her. She saw that her shoes were old and worn. Remembering when they were new, she reflected on how all things are transient and how quickly they change. "Soon," she thought, "I will be an old nun in this monastery." Reflecting on how precious each moment was, she reached down to straighten her shoes. Doing so she noticed that if she moved them to the left, then there would be space for another pair of shoes to the right of hers. Thinking of the other monks and nuns who were coming to the meditation hall, she gently pushed her shoes to the side. Happy, the new nun entered the meditation hall.

Breathing

A scholar came to the Abbess and explained, "I have spent a lifetime studying Buddhism and it has not helped me much. What am I missing? What is it I need to understand?"

To prepare the scholar for her answer, the Abbess sat silent for a while. Then she said, "Breathe in an easy and relaxed way and then study what causes you to lose that ease. Everything you really need to know about Buddhism will be found in that investigation."

The Real Dog

To learn how to direct the new monks and nuns, the Abbess would send them on a two-hour hike up the mountain to gather wild mushrooms from an isolated valley. On the way, they would have to pass the haunts of a wild dog. How the monastics reported their encounter with the dog revealed to the Abbess each novice's basic disposition.

Some novices would report that they had been too afraid to walk past the threatening dog. Some novices described the dog as being in distress and had wondered how they could help it. Others would happily come back with the mushrooms telling of the friendly dog they had met along the way. A few novices could say little about the dog, as in their determination to gather the mushrooms they had barely noticed the lazy dog resting next to the trail.

Sometimes the Abbess was asked which of these reports actually described the dog.

In reply, the Abbess would only smile.

Living by the Rules

The monastery librarian was an intelligent and inquisitive nun who had lived there for twenty-five years. She told this story about first coming to the monastery.

"As a young woman I was passionately interested in the truth. After years of unsuccessful searching I brought my quest to the monastery.

"When I asked the Abbess if she would ordain me so I could continue my quest in the monastery her response confused me and almost prompted me to leave.

"She said, 'If you want to be a nun here you must follow two rules. First, you must abandon any truth you discover. And second, you must never lie.'

"Perplexed but intrigued, I decided to try the monastic life under these rules. Before I could even begin I knew I first had to find the truth. When I finally started to have some inkling of what it is, I found it quite challenging to let go of it. I had a lot of doubt about the wisdom of doing so. But as I began to let go of it I found I felt lighter. I was also more apt to see situations fresh, without preconceived ideas. Dedicating myself to avoiding lying proved even harder to learn. I had no trouble with not speaking ordinary lies to others. I was much more challenged to learn how not to lie

to myself. But as I learned, this added to my sense of light-
ness and ease.

"By abandoning the truth and never lying, I eventually
found what I came to the monastery to find."

Noise and Silence

The monastery work leader always appeared peaceful. This was not so unusual among the monks and nuns of the monastery. He was unique, however, in that he remained peaceful and calm even when the monastery was at its busiest, for example when large crowds of people visited to celebrate the Buddha's birthday. If a person was needed to visit the hustle and bustle of the local market town, this was the monk the monastery usually sent.

When asked how he managed to remain peaceful, he said, "I entered the monastery for peace and quiet. I had spent years in the harried world of commerce and people. I longed for the silence the monastery was rumored to have.

"I was delighted with my first weeks in the monastery. The silence was exquisite. However, as I settled into the silence of the place, I was shocked to learn how noisy my own mind was. The real noise was within! It was the busyness of my own mind that oppressed me, not the noise and activity of the world.

"Now it doesn't matter to me where I go. I carry the silence within me. "

On Caffeine

O nce the Abbess said, "Desire and aversion are the caffeine of the soul. If you stop stimulating yourself with them it will take a few days to adjust. You may even go through a challenging period of withdrawal. But if you can successfully overcome your addiction to desire and aversion, you will discover your natural energy and clarity."

Listening

A young woman from another country moved with her family to live for one year in a town near the monastery. When, in the course of the year she discovered the monastery, she would periodically visit to have discussions with the Abbess. The Abbess introduced her to meditation, which became very meaningful for the young woman.

When the family's year-long stay was drawing to an end, the young woman asked the Abbess, "In my country there is no Buddhism and no one has even heard about meditation. How can I continue to learn and deepen the practice you have started me on?"

The Abbess said, "When you return home ask far and wide for who, among the wise people, is recognized as having the greatest ability to listen. Ask that person to instruct you in the art of listening. What you learn about listening from such a person will teach you how to further your meditation practice."

Doubt

A nun came to the Abbess complaining that doubt was her primary challenge along the Buddhist path. She had doubt about the path itself, about the teachings, about her teachers, and most importantly, about her own ability to succeed in the Buddhist practice.

"Your problem," said the Abbess, "is that you don't doubt enough. If you are going to the trouble of doubting, then continue your doubting, but do it more thoroughly. Please also doubt your doubt."

The Question

This monastery had a most unusual old monk. Seemingly senile, he had retired from the daily life of the monastery. He spent all his days in his little bedroom. During the day he sat quietly in a chair looking out the window. It was rare for him to speak. When food was delivered to his room he would not interrupt his window gazing to give any indication that he was aware that someone had entered his room. But it was rumored that he would speak to people who had reached an impasse in their spiritual life, provided the person approached him with sincerity. Many people came to the monastery seeking his counsel. However, most went away in disappointment, often concluding that the rumor was baseless and that the monk was indeed senile.

A local accountant was a longtime lay supporter of the monastery and a devotee of the Buddhist tradition. He came frequently to offer gifts of vegetables and to listen to the Abbess' Dharma talks. However, he remained an unhappy man.

One day when he came bearing vegetables, the Abbess asked the accountant if he would deliver lunch to the old monk. The accountant agreed, and remembering the rumor, hoped the monk would have something to say that would help him overcome his unhappiness.

Having never met the old monk, the accountant entered his bedroom reverently and was in awe of the stillness and peace permeating the room. He placed the lunch tray on the bed and then pulled up a chair to sit next to the monk. For a long time they sat looking out the window together. Then at some point the monk leaned over and turned toward the accountant in the way a person might lean forward to whisper a secret. The accountant froze as he gazed into the warm eyes of the monk who was looking directly at him.

The monk asked, "Why not?"

At first the accountant couldn't understand what was being said. So the monk kindly repeated, "Why not?"

A torrent of words came pouring out of the accountant's frightened mouth, "Not now......I am not ready......I have responsibilities......I am incapable..."

Softly, the monk asked again, "Why not?"

With that, the accountant ran out of the monastery, never to be seen again. And to this day, he is still running from that question.

Distractions

A young monk complained of having too many distractions to be able to meditate. He explained to the Abbess that he had tried every possible approach to overcome the distractions. He had redoubled his efforts at concentration. He had been diligent in trying to let the distractions go. He had also tried many antidotes, including ignoring them. When none of these approaches worked he even tried turning toward the distractions to include them as part of the meditation. He had also investigated the reactions, feelings, and beliefs he had in relation to the distractions. None of this had helped. He remained plagued.

"In that case, said the Abbess, "there remains only one thing for you to do. Please gaze upon the distractions with kindness and be still."

Beyond Here and Now

A mother of young children came to the Abbess and said, "A traveling teacher recently taught that all our difficulties will go away if we would be fully in the present moment. This can't be right. I watch my children and so often they are too much in the present moment. When it is time for school, they don't get ready because they're absorbed in whatever they are playing in the moment. When I walk them to school, they stop to enjoy the flowers, bugs, sticks and rocks they find along the way. My kids need to learn something else besides being in the moment; otherwise, I can't manage my job as a parent."

The Abbess replied, "It is unfortunate that some Buddhist teachers overemphasize the present moment. It is as if the present moment is their Buddhist God. It's true the present moment is the wellspring of all things good. However, if we aren't careful it can also be the wellspring for all things ill. The point of Buddhism is not to be in the present moment. The practice is to be aware of the present moment enough so we can address our clingings as they are occurring. Your kids know how to be present. But they are not old enough to notice how they get attached. As they get older they will become less focused on their present moment experience and if they are taught well, they will simultaneously become more and more aware of how they cling. Peace is found through not-clinging."

The Many Ways of Walking the Path

The monastery held a big public event celebrating the birth of the Buddha. As crowds of visitors came to commemorate the event, commotion and noise reigned throughout the monastery.

In the early afternoon, four young monks decided to slip out the back gate. They had determined that they weren't needed and that their absence would not be noticed. They decided to hike a well-trodden path into the mountains.

As they hiked, one of the monks said, "I am so glad we decided to get away from all the chaos of the monastery. I was agitated by all the people and activity."

Another monk replied, "It hadn't occurred to me that we were trying to get away from anything. I thought we left the monastery because we wanted to reach the outlook with the beautiful vista that is along this path."

The third monk then spoke up quite forcefully, "I am not interested in escaping what is behind us or focusing on distant goals. I thought we were simply walking the path to enjoy the views each step along the way."

Impatient with what the others had said, the fourth monk said, "I thought we headed out on this walk to get exercise. The goals you all have for our walk are all temporary. By building up our strength we will be better prepared for even longer hikes that we may have to undergo. Also, it is such a delight to move and feel vitality coursing through the body."

As each was committed to his approach for walking the path, they each decided to go their own way. After all, why should they be troubled to walk with someone who had a different understanding of what the walk was about?

The further he walked from the monastery, the less the first monk felt oppressed by the festivities he had left behind. When he felt quite removed from the monastery, his motivation for the hike disappeared and he sat down and took a nap leaning against a tree.

The second monk was so eager to reach the outlook that he didn't notice the rocks and roots that lay across the path. He stumbled and fell often. After a while he was scraped and bruised enough that he sat down, giving up on hiking further along the path.

When the path passed through a scenic meadow, the third monk left the path to admire the beautiful butterflies flying among the colorful flowers. Thoroughly enjoying himself, he stayed in the meadow until it was time to return to the monastery.

The fourth monk became absorbed in the exercise of walking. As the flow of vitality increased in his body, his attention was increasingly absorbed into his immediate physical experience. When the path went by the outlook, he didn't notice and kept hiking further into the mountains.

That evening, the Abbess—who tended to notice everything that happened at the monastery—met with the four monks to ask why they had left together but returned separately.

The monks explained that they had disagreed about why they were on the path. They said because they couldn't agree on what they were doing, they had separated, each hiking according to his own purpose for walking the path.

Upon hearing this, the Abbess laughed and then said, "The Buddhist Path only exists when someone walks it. While people walk on this Path for many different reasons, they are equally all walkers. It doesn't matter what motivates them, as long as they walk the Path mindfully. If you are mindful, the shortcomings of any purpose will be overcome. As Abbess, my job is to help make sure you keep walking the Path. Your mindfulness and persistence will take care of everything else."

The Sisters

I dentical twin sisters found their way to the monastery. At first it was very difficult to distinguish one from the other and the monks and nuns often confused them. Not only did they look the same, but they also had the same mannerisms, identical ways of talking and, as nuns, they wore the same robes. In addition, they both had extremely aversive personalities. They were astute observers who seemed always to see what was wrong.

But after some months, marked differences between them appeared. They remained as aversive as ever, however, one sister became more and more dour and discouraged. The other became increasingly happy. Soon enough the first sister left the monastic life, though this did nothing to improve her dark state. The second sister went on to become the guest master and many of the monastery guests remarked how her happiness was contagious.

The first sister directed her aversion outwardly; when she suffered all she could see was what was wrong with the world. The second sister looked inward when she suffered; she focused on being averse to her aversion and toward whatever clinging created it. The first sister was crushed by her aversion. The second was liberated by hers.

A MONASTERY WITHIN

Wisdom

The Doors Open Wide

Being Free

C omplaining he had too many difficulties to be able to discover real freedom, a monk told the Abbess, "My back hurts, the monastery is either too cold or too hot, the food doesn't taste good, and my work as the chief dish washer is very unpleasant."

The Abbess replied, "If you're free only when you are comfortable, then you are not really free."

On Wasting Time

A visiting monk once asked the Abbess, "How would I know if I am wasting my time?"

The Abbess replied, "If you are suffering."

The Right Question

A young man once appeared at the gates of the monastery with zeal and determination to be a monk. Asking permission to enter the monastery he was granted an interview with the Abbess.

The Abbess asked, "Why do you want to become a monk? Why do you wish to leave the world behind to engage in the Buddhist path?"

"I want to know who I am," was the man's earnest reply.

"'Who am I?' is the wrong question!" said the Abbess.

"But I have read books that explain that this is the great question! If one penetrates this question, one attains realization."

Ferociously the Abbess shot back, "Books, what do they know? Go away and come back with a real question! Come back with your question." With that the man was quickly ushered out of the monastery.

Thinking about this, the young man returned the next day and told the Abbess he had a better question.

"Let's hear it." said the Abbess.

"I want to discover the truth."

"That is not the right question. Out!" barked the Abbess.

The man hung his head, left and spent a few days thinking about what might be the right question. Returning to the monastery he said to the Abbess, "What is liberation?"

"Out."

Discouraged because his deep yearning for liberation had not been good enough, the young man began wandering around the country constantly searching. Sometimes he searched out the wisest people he could find and asked them what the 'right question' might be.

Periodically he returned to the monastery with a new question.

"How can I end my suffering?"

"Out."

"What is wrong with me?"

"Out."

"What can I do for you?"

"Out."

"What is THE QUESTION?"

"That is for you to discover. Out!"

"Why are you asking me for a question?"
"Out."

Though the Abbess continued to send the young man out of the monastery, it was not without feeling. Sometimes the man asked with such deep humility that when the Abbess barked "out," a teardrop would run down her cheek. This is what happened when the man asked,

"How can I discover love and compassion?
"Out."

"How can I be of service to others?"
"Out."

As the weeks, months and years passed by, more and more time elapsed between the young man's visits to the monastery. Searching for the right question became his quest. Only occasionally did he come across one he thought he could try with the Abbess. Then after asking the following question, he no longer returned to the monastery:

"What is happening now?"
"Out."

Some ten years after the man initially knocked on the monastery gate, the Abbess had the occasion to travel to some distant place. There she ran into the man, now not so young, who appeared unusually at peace. The Abbess asked him why he had stopped coming with a question.

"Oh, after some time I simply forgot to return. Everywhere I go and in everything I do I keep asking 'what is the question?' This quest has become more and more powerful for me. It fills my days and nights. It keeps me very present and interested. For a long time now I haven't thought about the monastery or about much else from my past. I now care less about answers than with discovering the question each situation calls forth."

"The Abbess smiled and said, "Now you may enter the monastery."

The man replied, "Thank you, but now I have no need to do so."

The Abbess bowed deeply and left.

The Miracle

The rumor spread around the country that the monastery was a place of miracles.

One day a university professor and religious skeptic stormed into the monastery demanding to see something miraculous.

"Your next breath," said the Abbess, "is a miracle."

The professor became speechless.

To Be Buddha

A nun once asked the Abbess, "Who was the Buddha really?

Smiling and leaning forward mischievously, the Abbess "Don't you already know?"

Confused by this answer to her question, the nun felt overwhelmingly self-conscious. She couldn't find the words to even say she didn't know.

The Abbess then explained, "To know who the Buddha is you have to start with something simple. Take breathing, for example. Like you right now, the Buddha breathed. When you are aware of your breathing, you are aware of physical experiences the Buddha knew as he breathed. When you see how your breaths arise and pass away, it is just as the Buddha saw his breaths arise and pass away.

"Like you right now, the Buddha experienced physical sensations in his body. When you see that the many sensations you experience through the day arise and pass away, it is just as the Buddha saw his sensations arising and passing.

"Like you right now, the Buddha experienced pleasant and unpleasant feelings. When you see directly how your experiences of pleasure and pain arise and pass away, it is just how the Buddha saw pleasure and pain come and go.

"Like you right now, the Buddha had thoughts. When you see those thoughts come and go, you are experiencing how the Buddha saw thoughts arise and pass away.

"Like you right now, the Buddha experienced particular states of mind. When you see your state of mind arise and pass, you are experiencing how the Buddha saw his mind states arise and pass away.

"Like you right now, the Buddha was aware of himself. When you see how your ideas of who you are arise and pass away, you are experiencing how the Buddha saw his ideas of self arise and pass away."

Hearing this, the nun became aware of her experience as it was happening in the present moment. In a way she never imagined possible, she felt physically close to the Buddha. Rather than someone who lived thousands of years ago, she sensed a timelessness in which no time separated her from the Buddha. "I understand," said the nun. "Is this all I need to know?"

In reply, the Abbess said, "No, there is one more thing. When you see clearly that clinging to breathing, sensations, feelings, thoughts, states of mind, and self also arises and passes away, then you will know who the Buddha is. Then you will be free."

The Meaning of Life

A nun once asked the Abbess, "What is the meaning of life?"

In reply, the Abbess asked, "What motivates your question?"

Thinking for a while, the nun said, "Fear."

"Resolve your fear," the Abbess said, "and you won't need an answer to the meaning of life."

On Problems

One evening the Abbess taught, "Your problems won't be solved in this monastery. They will be dissolved."

The Path

When arriving at the monastery new monks and nuns would commonly ask the Abbess for instruction on the Path of practice. If they were insistent enough about finding the Path, the Abbess would take them to a remote corner of the monastery garden where people seldom went. There she pointed them to a narrow walkway that disappeared into the bushes and trees. She told them, "You will find the Path at the end of this walkway." Then the old Abbess turned away, leaving each novice to walk on alone.

Intrigued, the new monastics set off in search of the Path. Before long, however, the trail took a sharp turn. When they rounded the corner they came face to face with a very large mirror. It blocked their way. Seeing their own image reflected in the mirror confused them. Some wondered, "Maybe I have taken the wrong path." Still, no matter how many times they tried to retrace their steps or start over, sooner or later they found the mirror blocking their way again.

More than a few assumed the mirror was placed on the trail to show them that the real Path was in them, not in the external world. This understanding frightened some and they ran away. Others collapsed in hopelessness. Some simmered in anger. Occasionally, someone would become so upset that they would hurl a heavy rock at their reflection. The mirror, however, was impervious. Each time they threw a rock at it the stone bounced back and struck them instead.

There were some monastics who lingered in front of the mirror, each gazing at his or her own likeness. It mesmerized and delighted them. Their conceit spilled over as they perceived themselves as somehow being the great Buddhist Path. And, of course, there were those novices who simply tried to walk around the mirror. Believing it blocked their way, they plunged headlong into the surrounding thicket of bushes only to emerge scratched and bloodied by an impenetrable web of thorns and undergrowth.

From time to time one of them would see his or her mother or father standing next to them in the reflection. This was an eerie sight, since they knew they were alone. At other times, their reflected image was obscured by crowds of people.

In due course, some of the monks and nuns calmed down enough to stop and look carefully into their reflection. For many it was the first time they ever really looked deeply into themselves. More than a few concluded that the mirror and the reflection were the end of the Path. Those who did ended up stuck for a very long time. Others, however, remembered the Abbess' directive about finding the Path at the "end of this walkway." When these monks and nuns stopped and looked deeply into their likeness in the mirror, a wonderful realization arose in their minds. "The reflection is of me, but I am not the reflection." Then when they reached out and lightly touched the mirror, it gave way. Like a great door silently swinging open, it revealed a bright, expansive, sunlit section of garden unlike anything they could ever have imagined existed. Just beyond, at the edge of the path, stood the old Abbess holding two shovels.

The Abyss

A monk told this story:

"I had reached an impasse after twenty-five years in the monastery. I had devoted myself diligently to monastic practice. Through much effort my powers of concentration, mindfulness, and compassion were among the strongest the Abbess had ever seen. I was known for my peace and equanimity. I had no obvious attachments.

"However, I had not yet attained realization. Other monks and nuns, with less time in the monastery and less thorough practice had reached various levels of awakening. Everyone thought my circumstance was most strange.

"Then one day the Abbess took me aside for a long talk. We discussed how I was held back by my fear of completely letting go. As much as I trusted the spiritual life, at my core was some deep, unarticulated nagging mistrust. As long as I could remember, a part of me was on the lookout for impending tragedy. At the end of the conversation the Abbess told me she could think of only one more catalyst for my enlightenment. Just the possibility brought me tears of joy ... until she told me it meant entering a basement room called 'the Abyss'.

"No one in many generations had entered this room.

Only the Abbess was entrusted with the secret knowledge of what was inside. No one else knew. While the red door to the room was kept locked, it didn't need to be. An atmosphere of terror emanated from within and the monks and nuns were afraid to walk anywhere near the door.

"Walking down to the basement the Abbess explained that my one and last opportunity was inside this room. Once I entered this room, there would be no turning back. Standing in front of the door I had mixed feelings about entering. The Abbess carefully explained the instructions that had been transmitted to her. I was to step into the room. The Abbess would close and lock the door behind me and under no circumstance would she unlock it again. On entering the room I was simply to walk to the other side of the room and exit through the door there. It sounded easy enough.

"Suddenly, the Abbess opened the door and pushed me inside. Before I could get my bearings, I heard the door lock behind me.

"The room proved to be huge, perhaps 100 feet wide. On the other side of the room was a door just like the one I had entered.

"The room had no floor. I was standing on a two foot ledge as wide as the door. Between me and the other door was a gaping abyss. I could not see the bottom. From the depths came horrible grinding and cracking sounds. Occasionally a ball of flame shot upward.

"I was scared and perplexed. How was I supposed to walk across? I spent the first day standing on the ledge studying the room, certain that I was meant to discover some secret way to get across. I spent the second day banging on the door hoping that someone would let me out. I cried most of the third day until, while sitting on the ledge, one of my slippers fell off my foot. As it fell the grinding noises seemed to get worse.

"On the fourth day I desperately and repeatedly reviewed the instructions. They were so simple: Walk across the room and out the other door. Could I trust the Abbess?

"Tired and hungry, on the fifth day I gave up all hope. Convinced I had no other choice but to try the instructions, I decided to walk out off the ledge. I tried not to imagine what awaited me down in the depths. Terrified, I looked straight ahead and took a step into the room, into the unknown. As my foot came down, the ledge stretched forward, receiving me with a firm, stable base.

"It took me another day to take the second step, but when I finally did, the ledge again extended itself outwards to receive my foot. I continued walking into the emptiness and with each step the ledge became longer. Soon enough I had reached the opposite side.

"From that day on, letting go into the freedom of realization has come easily."

A Day Without Self

One evening the Abbess declared that the next day every monk and nun was prohibited from using the words "I", "me", "mine" and "myself" unless it was required for answering a direct question from someone else.

The next morning was chaotic. Feeling as if they were learning to walk all over again, the monastics kept tripping over their words and stumbling in all their interpersonal interactions.

By the afternoon some were humbled, confused or dismayed to learn how frequently their impulses to speak as well as their thinking were self-referential.

By the evening the predominant atmosphere in the monastery was one of relief as the monks and nuns realized that they had survived an entire day without initiating any self-focused discussion.

And as they lay themselves down to sleep, each person was amazed at how clear and at ease their mind had become.

On Not Self

A t the end of a detailed discussion of the Buddhist teaching on self and not-self, the Abbess paused and then concluded,

"We are so alone, we are not even here to keep ourselves company."

The monastics weren't sure they understood what the Abbess meant. Later when they asked her, she replied "The not-self teaching can be challenging until you realize that there is no one who is challenged."

The True Self

A woman came to the monastery determined to ask the Abbess how she could discover her true self. She had assumed many identities over her lifetime, most of them identities others had expected her to have.

When she presented her concern, the Abbess replied, "Since knowing the true self is so important for you, you should ask this question of someone who has fully penetrated this issue. We have a very learned monk here who has read every Buddhist scripture and the many commentaries. He has studied with some of the greatest Buddhist teachers of this age. He has spent years meditating and has deep realization. Come, I will introduce you to him."

The Abbess led the woman into the courtyard where a solitary monk was absorbed in sweeping. "That is him," said the Abbess. "When you're interested in the true self it's important not to be abstract. Don't ask what the true self is, ask him what *his* true self is."

Shyly, but with great hope, the woman walked up to the monk and asked, "What is your true self?"

The monk smiled and continued to sweep.

Going back to the Abbess the woman said, "He didn't answer my question."

"Quite the opposite," replied the Abbess. "He gave you the most precise answer he could at this time. When he sweeps, his true self is the sweeping."

On Suchness

G iving instruction for meditation, the Abbess once held up a rose in her right hand. "Please look at this flower," she said. "Notice its suchness, how it appears in and of itself."

Continuing to hold up the rose in her right hand, with her left hand she held up a little dandelion. "Now we can say something about the rose we couldn't say before. Now we can say that the rose is the large flower compared to the dandelion which is the small flower."

Putting down the dandelion, the Abbess picked up a large sunflower. "While nothing has changed for the rose itself, we can now say the rose is the small flower compared to the sunflower."

"Large and small are not inherent in the rose. Large and small reside in the comparison with other flowers. Freed of comparison, a flower is just itself.

"Gaze directly at your own suchness. Much of the suffering you will have in life will arise from comparative thinking. In meditation don't compare yourself with anything. There is no need to compare yourself to others, ideals, past experiences or future imaginations. Residing in suchness you will find the path to peace."

It Is All Empty

T he janitor was one of the more radiant monks in the monastery. His peace and joy inspired everyone who met him. Never seeming to want anything, he had a knack for being in the right place at the right time when others needed help. He was always thorough in doing his job and no one had ever seen him bothered by anything.

One day he was asked if monastic life had ever been difficult. This is what he said:

"Before coming to the monastery, my life was very hard. I considered ending my life because my suffering was so great. For me the monastery was the end of the road. I saw it as my last chance. When I first arrived I had a long interview with the Abbess. She asked me lots of questions. I told her things about my life that I had never revealed to anyone. At the end of the interview she welcomed me to the monastery. As I took my leave, I asked what sort of spiritual practice I should undertake. The Abbess looked up at me with such compassion and confidence that I thought she was preparing to tell me something very important. But all she said was, "Always walk completely through the doors."

"For the rest of that day I wondered if I had heard correctly. How could walking through doors be helpful advice to someone as despondent as me? Perhaps the old woman was becoming senile.

"The next day, to my surprise, the monastery doors started talking to me. Every time I went through a door I heard a faint whisper. At first I thought I was imagining it so I didn't give it much attention. But when the whispering kept reoccurring, I strained to hear what was being said. Finally, I was able to make out the words. It seemed each door was whispering the same thing: 'It is all empty.'

"I asked the other monks if they too heard the voices, but none did. I asked them if they knew the meaning of 'It is all empty.' They just smiled and shrugged their shoulders, as if they didn't have a clue.

"Pretty quickly I decided that the voices were a reminder of the life I had left behind. All my possessions, along with the endless pursuits I had run after, the burning drive for recognition, the insatiable womanizing; all of that was indeed empty. The whispering doorways seemed to be reassuring me that I had made the right decision in coming to the monastery. They were reminding me that no longer was there anything outside the monastery walls for me to go after.

"So at first the voices made me happy. Convinced that

the world I left behind was shallow, I threw myself whole-heartedly into the monastic routine. What a delight it was to have finally found a meaningful life! But as the doorways continued to whisper 'It is all empty,' I began to have doubts about monastic life as well. Was this life also hollow, meaningless? Adding to my concerns, the voices started to grow louder.

"Before long I felt as much despair about monastic life as I had about my previous life. Trying to find something that would give meaning and purpose to my life, I decided to devote more time to meditation and thereby develop my inner life. Certainly the pursuit of real spiritual attainments would be meaningful.

"The meditation practice seemed to lighten my despair, and when my meditations were deep I was filled with confidence. I began to feel quite happy, even happy-go-lucky. I had found the key to happiness and was convinced that I was surpassing all the other monks in holiness. But every time I left the meditation hall the doors whispered again, 'It is all empty.'

"After a while this began to grate on me. I became increasingly angry because the voices seemed to suggest that my newfound identity as a deeply spiritual person was empty. When the anger became too much to bear, I was forced to admit that I had been caught in pride and that my vanity too was empty.

"Once the anger passed, I carried on with my mediation practice. After all, nothing else seemed to make sense. Then the voices starting commenting on the meditation itself. I heard again 'It is all empty.' Did this mean that meditation itself was meaningless?

"My despair returned with a vengeance. I tried hiding in my room so I wouldn't have to go through any doors. I took to climbing through windows whenever possible. If I did have to pass through a door, I ran through trying to distance myself from the voices. By now the voices had grown very loud. As I ran down the halls the phrase 'It is all empty' echoed after me.

"After a while, every thought I had, every wish I hoped for, and every effort I made was assaulted by 'It is all empty' resonating throughout the monastery. I couldn't take it anymore. I ran toward the front gate of the monastery intending to find a tall mountain cliff and throw myself off. It no longer made sense to keep on living if life was going to be so hard. But as I came to the front gate the doors loomed large in front of me. I was too frightened to pass through them. I felt I couldn't survive one more voice telling me that 'It is all empty.'

"I stood there, frozen for a long time, but then I remembered the practice the old Abbess had given me on my first day in the monastery: "Always walk completely through the doors." The instruction seemed so useless the first time I heard it. Now it seemed monumental. I could not manage to get myself to pass through the front gate.

"Inside my head, a voice kept repeating 'It is all empty. It is all empty.' My mind couldn't find any object to rest on because when it did I was reminded that it too was empty. My mind became increasingly contracted, turning in on itself. It kept pulling away from everything until all that was left was the frightened mind itself. Then, one last time, a voice boomed out, 'It is all empty,' and with that I let go of my mind.

"Since that day the voices stopped and I've never again worried about the meaning of anything. Neither despair nor hope is relevant for me. Happily, emptiness permeates everything."

On Seeking

Once, teaching the monastics, the Abbess told this story:

"There was a species of humans born in the ocean. They were born being able to swim and all their life they swam. After many years of constantly swimming one man started to get tired. He heard that if he swam far enough to the east he would find a resting place that was free of the ocean.

"After swimming east for many years and not finding the resting place, someone told him of a rumor of such a place in the south. He swam south for more years but never found it. Similarly he swam to the north and to the west but nowhere could he find the mythic place.

"Bone weary from his endless swimming he came across a woman who laughed at his quest. "The rest you seek is not found anywhere else than where you are. All you have to do is turn over on your back and float".

"Monks and nuns, desires are endless! You won't get to the end of desire by desiring. What you seek is not found through seeking. When you can let go fully, and simply float, it is right here."

Awakening

The Abbess once said,
"If a person is always surrounded by music she may never imagine there is an alternative. But if, after many years, she comes to a place where there is no music she may be surprised, maybe even shocked, by the relief of not hearing the constant sound.

"If her experience of silence makes a strong enough impression, then when she returns to the world of music she will not only hear the music but also the silence which is always here with the music.

"With Awakening you will know a peace which is always here".

A MONASTERY WITHIN

Epilogue

Sheltering Others

Who's Enlightened

A young monk asked the Abbess:
"How can I recognize if someone is enlightened?"

The Abbess replied, "The first thing to consider is if they are helpful to other beings."

Stories

An old monk traveled from afar seeking advice from the Abbess.

He explained that all his life he had used stories to tell himself and others who he was. He lived in some stories for decades. When eventually a story proved hollow and meaningless he would find another belief, another religion, another role.

He told the Abbess, "Buddhism and being a monk has been my story for the last thirty years, but now I've let go of even that story. With no story I don't know who I am. How can I live when I don't have a story?"

Gently the Abbess said to him, "This is good. Now, turn to the people around you and listen to their stories."

ABOUT THE AUTHOR

Gil Fronsdal never had the slightest interest in writing stories until he had been a Buddhist teacher for 15 years. It was then he discovered Buddhism can sometimes be more effectively taught through stories than direct explanations. Before becoming a teacher for the Insight Meditation Center in Redwood City, California, Gil spent years practicing in Buddhist monasteries and meditation centers in the United States, Japan, and Southeast Asia. He also received a PhD in Buddhist Studies from Stanford University. In retrospect, he now realizes he wrote his dissertation on stories connected to ancient Buddhist ideals of compassion and liberation.

Gil's teachings can be found at www.audiodharma.org and www.insightmeditationcenter.org/books-articles/. His translation of the *Dhammapada*, an important collection of Buddhist verses, is published by Shambhala Publications. He is also the author of *The Issue at Hand*, a collection of essays on mindfulness practice.

Gil is married and has two sons who are the source of many stories.

ACKNOWLEDGEMENTS

To all the people I have practiced the Dharma with, I express my profound gratitude. I especially offer my thanks to those with whom I shared monastic life.

This book would not have come to be without the support and encouragement of others. I offer a deep bow of gratitude to Diana Clark for being a wonderful editor. Without her editing skill, suggestions and encouragement I wouldn't have found my way out of these stories. I also offer a deep bow of gratitude to Elena Silverman who spent so much time skillfully designing and laying out the book. It was a great pleasure to work with her. I also bow in gratitude to Ines Freedman and Nona Olivia for their encouragement and suggestions. I am grateful to Mary Grace Orr who advised me to write stories of nuns after the first stories were only about monks. I also thank my family for their support. Without the encouragement, confidence and editing my wife Tamara Kan provides, this book and so much more would not be possible. My son Toren provided important suggestions and creative samples for the design of the book. And my son Kai was a living example of the wonder that gives birth to many of the stories.

Made in United States
Troutdale, OR
07/06/2023

11011750R10067